TEACHING WITH
OBJECT LESSONS

TEACHING WITH OBJECT LESSONS

By

DOROTHY HARRISON PENTECOST

MOODY PRESS

CHICAGO

This book is lovingly dedicated
to My Mother

CONTENTS

7

UNDERSTANDING THE WORD

PREPARATION: Secure a foreign newspaper, or a letter written in a foreign language. Foreign newspapers can be bought at a downtown newsstand in any city.

PRESENTATION

I brought a newspaper with me this morning, and I want one of you, who is a good reader, to come up here and help me by reading some of the news in the paper. Thank you, Jim. Here is the paper. What is the matter? Why don't you read it? Oh, it is written in a language that you don't understand! But it is written in letters of our alphabet. You learned the alphabet when you went to school, didn't you? Then why can't you understand what is written in the newspaper? Of course, you can't read it. I didn't expect you to. I can't read it myself. Why can't we read it? We can't read it because it is written in a foreign language. We have never been trained to read in Spanish.

What would we have to do to know what is in this newspaper? That is right! We would have to find someone who could read Spanish, and he could read it to us so we would understand it, and if there were any things that we didn't understand about Mexico he could also explain them to us. We need someone who knows and understands Spanish and English to teach us what is in the newspaper.

God's Word says the Bible is like a foreign newspaper to unsaved people. All the letters are there and even the words that they can read in English, but they can never know the true message of the Bible by themselves (I Cor. 2:14). All the education of all the colleges in the world can't give a person a true understanding of the message of the Bible. Then, how can we really understand the Bible? We must have someone who understands to teach us from our Bibles. Our teacher is the Holy Spirit (I Cor. 2:10-13). The Holy Spirit was the One who moved men to write the Bible and told them what to write. Since the Holy Spirit is the

Author, or Writer, of the Bible, He certainly can tell us the things that are written in it (I Cor. 2:10).

If the Holy Spirit is sent to be our Teacher, then why is it that some people can't understand the Bible? Let me read you a verse. (Read I Cor. 2:14. Use the word UNSAVED instead of NATURAL.) The people who have never taken the Lord Jesus Christ as their Saviour don't have the Holy Spirit in their hearts to teach them the deep things of God from the Word. The verse says that it is all foolishness to them because it can be understood only as the Holy Spirit teaches it to us.

The first thing is to be sure that you have been saved by asking the Lord Jesus to come into your heart. If you haven't done that, won't you do it right now? All you have to do is ask Him to save you. As soon as you do that, the Holy Spirit comes into your heart to be there always. Then each time you read your Bible or hear the Word taught, just ask God to help you listen to the Holy Spirit as He makes the message plain to you.

A JUMP

PREPARATION: No preparation is necessary for this lesson.

PRESENTATION

You can't see the object I brought for our lesson this morning because several of you are going to be my object lesson. I want two boys and two girls to come up here to help me. Thank you. Stand right beside me, shoulder to shoulder. Now, I want each of you in turn to jump across the room. Oh, you don't think you can do it? Well, each of you can try and I'll make a little chalk mark to see how far each of you jumped. (Let each jump in turn and mark where they jumped.) Now you may sit down. (Compare the distances each one jumped.) Dan jumped farther than the rest of you, but even he didn't jump across the room as I told him to do, did he? So, you don't think that anyone can

12

jump that far? I don't either. Some of you jumped a little way and some of you jumped farther, but no one could jump all the way across the room.

God has asked us to do something that none of us can do. He says that we have to be holy and sinless. We all know that we are sinners and sin everyday. We aren't perfect, and we can't make ourselves righteous no matter how much we try. Let's see what God's Word says. (Read Rom. 6:23.) It says that ALL have sinned and come short of the glory of God, just as these children came short of jumping across the room as I required of them, even though they tried as hard as they could. So God says that no matter how hard we try or what we do, we can't be as holy as He is.

God knew that we couldn't because we have a sin nature in us that makes us want to sin. God loves us so much that He planned a way to make us righteous. The Lord Jesus Christ came down here on the earth to die for us. Salvation is a free gift (Eph. 2:8-10). All we have to do is to ask Him to come into our hearts. He wants to come into our hearts but He won't force His way in. We have to ask Him to come in. After we let Christ in our hearts, He forgives our sins. But He does even more than that. He gives us His righteousness, so what God sees is not our sin but Christ's righteousness. This is the only way we can measure up to God's glory.

If I required you to jump across the room, you couldn't do it. But if I carried you across the room without your feet touching the floor, you would have done what I required. Now, God says that we have all come short of His glory, but He gave us the Lord Jesus Christ to die for us so we can have the righteousness that He requires by taking Christ as our Saviour. Christ did for us what it is impossible for us to do for ourselves. This way there is nothing required of us but to take Christ as Saviour. Won't you do that right now, if you haven't already done it?

FILTHY RAGS

PREPARATION: Put a dirty, torn towel, that has been used as a dust cloth, in a box.

PRESENTATION

I want to show you a gift that I brought with me this morning. Look! Would you give this towel to your mother or to a friend? Why wouldn't you? It is dirty and ragged and useless! When we give gifts to people we love, we want to give them the nicest things that we can afford. I am afraid that your mother would be very hurt to receive something like this. You'd be ashamed to give this towel to anyone.

There are some people who are hurting and insulting God by offering things to Him that are worse than this old towel. Let me read you what the Bible has to say about it. (Read Isa. 64:6a.) Everything good that we try to offer to God for our salvation is like old, dirty rags in

15

His sight. No matter how good we try to be, it is worse than nothing to God. Joining the church, being baptized, giving money to God's work, etc., are nothing in God's sight but useless rags. God is trying to teach us that apart from the work of the Lord Jesus Christ there is nothing we can do that will please God. We will only be insulting Him as we would insult a friend to whom we gave this old towel. What would your mother do with a gift like this? (Show old towel again.) She would just throw it away. She couldn't hang this in the bathroom for anyone to use.

Just so God has no use for anything that we try to offer Him for a way to Heaven. In fact, God won't receive anything we offer. He refuses even to see what we are trying to do. We can be very happy indeed that God doesn't require us to do anything to have our sins forgiven and to make a way to Heaven. We could never do enough to work our way into Heaven, and we could never do anything that would wash away our sins. But God loves us so much that He has provided another way for us to be saved and accepted by Him. He sent the Lord

Jesus Christ to die on the cross for us. Jesus Christ paid the price for everyone when He died. When we ask Him to come into our hearts to save us, He not only washes away our sin for us, but He does something about the "filthy rags" of our righteousness that we tried to use to pay for our sins. Our sins are forgiven and we are given the righteousness of Christ for our own. (Read II Cor. 5:21.) Now God looks at us through this wonderful, new righteousness of Christ. All this is done for us and given to us as a free gift. We can't work for this and we can't do anything to pay God for it. This only comes from taking Christ as Saviour (Eph. 2:8-10.) After we are saved, then we can work for God because we love Him and appreciate what He has done for us. God has a plan for our lives. We want to find that plan and do it to His glory. Don't try to offer God anything for your salvation. Just take Jesus Christ as your Saviour and He will do it all for you.

A CAKE

PREPARATION: Take the ingredients, mentioned in the lesson, to make a cake. If possible, take a finished cake and give the children a treat after the lesson, or take a picture of a cake. A cake recipe may be substituted for the things mentioned above.

PRESENTATION

I have brought a lot of objects with me this morning for our lesson. Here I have all the ingredients for making a cake. You know how sweet and tasty and good a cake is, but did you ever think about all the things your mother uses to make a cake? Did you even taste flour? It is tasteless and feels like powder in your mouth. Vanilla gives a cake a nice flavor, but when you put some on your tongue it is very bitter. This chocolate is bitter too when eaten by itself, because this is not the sweet kind you eat in candy bars. Eggs are so slimy when they are beaten that I can't eat them. Some people can drink them with milk. In fact about the only things that go into a cake that are good by themselves are the sugar and milk. After all these things are mixed together, the batter is put in a hot oven to bake before we can eat it.

(Read Ps. 37:23.) We know that God has a plan for us and that plan is made in His love and wisdom. He decides what is best for each one of us. We also are told that all things in God's plan for us are working together for good to those who belong to the Lord Jesus Christ. The reason God sends different events into our lives is to conform us to Christ, to make us more like Christ (Rom. 8:28). Sometimes we need hard, bitter experiences like being disappointed in not getting the grades we expected at school, or being sick in bed for a long time, just as the vanilla and the chocolate are necessary for the cake. Maybe God sees that not having a vacation trip, or having to help at home, are what you need to make you more like

Christ, so He sends experiences like this slimy egg that are hard to take. Other times He might send things that aren't interesting or exciting. Life seems dull, flat and tasteless like the flour. Often we have fun and good times like the sugar and milk in our cake. At times, God has to make some people go through such hard testings that might compare to the heat of the oven on our cake.

God knows that we need help to grow in Christ Jesus and that the only way we'll keep close to Him is through something hard we have to bear in our lives. There are things we like, and there are things so very unpleasant we don't like and pray that God will take them away. But we know that God says we should be thankful for everything He sends because He knows what is best for us to have.

When the cake ingredients are all mixed together and baked according to the recipe in my cook book, it will come out a beautiful, good-tasting cake just like this one. (Show cake or a picture of one.) When we are called on to bear something hard, just remember the cake recipe and that God has a plan for our lives too.

If we follow that plan we will have a wonderful, full and useful life that will please both God and us.

SHOES

PREPARATION: Get different kinds and sizes of shoes to take with you.

PRESENTATION

Here are some different kinds of shoes. This pair was worn by a child who was just learning to walk. This pair was worn by a boy who plays basketball in them. This pair of shoes belongs to a father when he goes to work, and here is a pair of high-heeled evening shoes that a mother wears when she is all dressed up for an evening out. All of you have on a pair of shoes this morning; so do I. Shoes are a very important part of our dress. Usually we put on our shoes in the morning before we start walking around the house, and very few people would walk outdoors without any shoes. Shoes always make us think of walking, don't they?

If your mother is anything like the mothers

22

I know, they have a lot to say about walking too. Has your mother said, "Don't walk in the street. Don't walk in the water; you'll get your feet wet. Always walk on the sidewalk. Walk facing the traffic so you can see if a car is coming"? Maybe she has to tell you to walk straight and not to slump. I can tell from your smiles that your mothers have said some of these things.

In the Bible, God compares the Christian life to a "walk." Even though we may all walk in different sizes and kinds of shoes, God says that we must all walk the same way as Christians to live a life that is pleasing to Him. He has given us lots of verses to tell us just how we are to walk as Christians.

Perhaps the most important verse that tells us how to walk to please God is Galatians 5:16. (Read the verse.) This verse means that we are to walk with the help of the Holy Spirit every minute of everyday, and then we do not sin and displease God. In the verses that follow, all the terrible sins are listed that we might do if we don't let the Holy Spirit help us live the Christian life. Then it lists all the wonderful things that the Holy Spirit will put in our lives if we will just let Him (Gal. 5:22, 23). When we have these things in us, then we know that the Holy Spirit is having His way in our lives. If these things are not in us, then we know that something is keeping the Holy Spirit from doing His work through us.

There are many other verses that tell us how we are to walk as Christians, but we can only talk about a few of them today. We are told that we should walk as Christ walked (I John 2:6). Christ is to be our example, or pattern for our lives. By studying the Bible, we can find out how Christ lived and copy His life. We are also told that we are to walk worthy of God because He has saved us and let us become His dear children (I Thess. 2:12). Our lives should be very different from the way they were before we were saved because we belong to God. We don't want to hurt God and make Him ashamed of the way we live. We are told to walk "circumspectly," redeeming the time because everything around us is evil (Eph. 5:15, 16). "Circumspectly" means to "look all around us." just as we do when we cross a busy street, so that we won't fall into a temptation to sin. We are to walk honestly, especially before the unsaved, so that we will be a witness to them (I Thess. 4:12). We are to walk in love (Eph. 5:2). We are supposed to love one another as Christ has loved us and given Himself as our Saviour. By seeing our love for both the saved and the unsaved, we are showing to the world that we belong to a God of love. We are to walk by faith and not by sight (II Cor. 5:7). Our faith is to be in the Lord Jesus Christ and not in anything that we can do. Then, we are not to walk as the unsaved walk. Our lives are to be so different from those who don't know Christ, that anyone can see at once that we are Christians (Eph. 4:17). The Holy Spirit is the only One who can help us walk in all these ways.

WALKING

PREPARATION: Take a cane, a piece of an old cast, or a crutch with you.

PRESENTATION

We have talked about shoes and about walking in a way that is pleasing to God. Today we want to learn just how God helps us walk the way He requires us to walk. I have brought a crutch with me. Do you know why people use these? They use them when something is wrong with their legs and they need extra help to walk. They put their weight on the crutch instead of on their legs. Have you ever had a broken leg or knew someone who had a broken leg? Usually, the doctor puts a cast on it to keep the leg and the bones straight, and then he lets the person walk with a cane or a crutch. Without this support the person would fall everytime he tried to walk.

26

One day a little girl went out to play in the snow. There was ice all over the sidewalk. She thought it would be fun to walk on the ice. She started out gaily but soon slipped and fell down. After that she asked her daddy to hold her hand so she wouldn't fall. She had learned that she couldn't walk on the ice without someone to hold her hand to keep her from falling.

God knew that even after we are saved, we would fall into sin unless we have someone to hold our hand and to help us. He gave us the Holy Spirit to be "the One called alongside to help." God has asked us to live a holy life and He knew that we couldn't do it ourselves. He gave us the Holy Spirit to live that life for us.

The Holy Spirit is God, just as God the Father and God the Son are. When the Lord Jesus Christ was here on earth, He told the disciples that He was going to die on the cross and then go back to Heaven after His resurrection. Their hearts were very sad because they were used to being with Christ and having His help. Christ made a wonderful promise to them and to all Christians who would live afterwards. He promised that He would send another Comforter (John 14:16). He was to take over the work that Christ had been doing for them while He was here on earth. He was to guide them, to comfort them, to strengthen them, to help them, and to teach them out of God's Word (John 14:26). The Holy Spirit is like the Lord Jesus Christ, and He was going to do just the same things for them that Christ had been doing. He can be with all Christians at the same time, and help all of us at the same time. Christ could be only with a few people at one time when He was here in His earthly body. If Christ lived today, we would probably never be able to see Him because we wouldn't have the money to make a trip to Palestine where He lived. But now the Holy Spirit has come in His place, and the Holy Spirit lives in the heart of every believer in every country of the world.

Christ also promised that the Holy Spirit would abide or be with us forever. He will never leave us or forsake us, no matter what we do. The minute you take Christ as your Saviour, the Holy Spirit is given to you and He comes to live in your heart (John 14:17). But we can hurt Him and keep Him from doing His work in our hearts by sinning. Every time we sin the Holy Spirit convicts us, or tells us that we have sinned. We must listen to Him and confess that sin as soon as He tells us what is wrong. Then God will forgive us and the Holy Spirit can go back to His work of teaching, guiding, and producing His fruit in our lives. And the Holy Spirit can help and support us in our Christian lives, just as a cane and a crutch help to support people who have something wrong with their legs.

When you see someone with a cane or a crutch, I hope it will remind you that you can't walk pleasing to God unless you let the Holy Spirit help and support. If you try to walk the Christian life without Him, you will fall into sin, just as people with broken legs will fall without a cane or crutch and a cast.

A STRONG HOLD

PREPARATION: No preparation is necessary for this lesson. The illustration is suggested in the lesson.

PRESENTATION

I didn't bring an object with me this morning because one of you is going to show me the object. One of you boys will help me. Stand here beside me. Do you know what a strong hold is, Jim? Will you take a strong hold on me to show just what you mean. (Be prepared for anything from a tight hold on your hand to a grab around your waist.) You are really strong, for when you were holding me I couldn't get loose no matter how much I tried. Now we all know what a strong hold is. It is such a tight hold that the one being held can't get away. Thank you, Jim. Now you may sit down.

God's Word tells us that God is a strong hold

for us. (Read Nahum 1:7.) When we are in trouble, God's hold is so strong that we can't fall and we can't be lost. We don't want to get away, do we? Have you ever had to have a tooth pulled or some stitches taken in your finger? You wanted someone to hold your hand while you were going through those things. Every time the doctor gives my little girls shots, they ask me to hold their hands. I always am glad to do it because I know that it helps them stand the pain. God says that He is our strong hold, and He will be always with us to help us through any pain or trouble or trial that we may have. The Lord Jesus Christ suffered everything that we will ever know when He was down here on earth. Do you know why He did that? The Bible tells us that He suffered all the testings and temptations that any man could suffer, so that He could help us when we are going through them (Heb. 2:18).

The Lord is so good to us all the time. We often hear people talk about how good the Lord is to them when everything is working out just as they want it to work. Did you ever hear anyone talk about how good the Lord is when they

are ill, or have lost a loved one, or something
else has gone wrong in their lives? God is good
all the time, and He cares for us in His goodness. It is His goodness that sends just the
things into our lives that He knows we need to
make us more like Christ. So we should be able
to say with all our hearts that God is good, no
matter what He sees fit to send into our lives.

Nahum 1:7 says that God knows the ones
who trust in Him. God really knows everyone
and everything, doesn't He? Yes, then what do
you think He means by this part of the verse?
He means that He knows us in a special way
as His own dear children through the Lord
Jesus Christ. I know all of you boys and girls
because you have been in this class for some
time, but I know my own two girls better than
I know you. They are my children and I have
been with them everyday and night since they
were born. I want all the best things in life for
them because they are my children. So God has
special things for those children who are His.

This is wonderful, but it is given to those who
trust in Him. That means the same thing as
believe. Only those who have believed in the

Lord Jesus Christ, and have taken Him as their Saviour, can take this promise as their own. If you have never taken Christ as your Saviour, wouldn't you like to do it right now? Just bow your head and say in your heart, "Dear Jesus, I believe that You died for me. Please come into my heart and save me." If you prayed that prayer and you really meant what you said, He has come into your heart and He will never leave you again! Then He will be your strong hold all the time.

HIDDEN IN CHRIST JESUS

PREPARATION: Hide something before the children arrive. The safest place is somewhere on your person. A piece of money in your shoe would be hard for them to find.

PRESENTATION

Do you have some special treasures of your very own that you keep hidden? When I was a little girl, I found a hollow place between two large roots of a tree. It was big enough to put a box in it, and that was where I kept all the things I didn't want anyone else to see or find.

I have hidden something in this room this morning before any of you got here. You can guess where it is, but the only way you can know where it is would be for me to tell you. I am sure that you can't find it by yourself, and until I tell you where it is and you find it, you won't know what I have hidden.

Did you know that God tells us in His Word that He has something hidden too? He calls it a mystery and by that He means it is a secret, and until we find it we don't know what it is. Just as I have told you that I have something hidden. But now, God is telling us that everyone can know this secret. Let me read Colossians 2:3. Now we know what God has hidden. He has hidden "all the treasures of wisdom and knowledge" about Himself. In whom has He hidden this knowledge? It is in the Lord Jesus Christ. The only way we can know God is to know the Lord Jesus Christ first. You remember that Christ said, "No man cometh unto the Father, but by me" (John 14:6). First, we must let the Lord Jesus Christ come into our hearts to save us. Then when He comes in, He will reveal, or tell us, all about God.

If you are unsaved, you may hear about God, but you can't really know Him. You may read the Bible and hear someone teach it, but you can't understand the message that God has for us in it. You can't talk to God in prayer and have His promise that He will answer unless you first belong to the Lord Jesus Christ. You can't live a Christian life unless you are saved, because to live a Christian life means that we are letting Christ live through us.

No matter how much education you have, or how many teachers you have, you can't know about God unless you have the Lord Jesus Christ in your heart to teach you about God. It is God's plan that all knowledge about Himself and His Word are hidden in Christ, and only when we have Christ can we know God and know what is written in His Word.

(Note: After the lesson is over, show the children what you have hidden and where it was hidden. Usually they will try to guess during the lesson.)

A HAT BOX

PREPARATION: Take a pretty hat in a hat box.

PRESENTATION

See, I have covered this hat box with the prettiest material that I could find. Several people who have seen me carry this hat box have said it is the most beautiful one that they have seen. Can you guess what I have inside? (Open the box and show the hat.) I see some of you were afraid to say "a hat" because that was so obvious. Yes, it is a hat. This is the prettiest one I have. It doesn't cover much of my head and isn't much good for keeping my head warm. That isn't the reason I wear it. I wear it to make me look as pretty as possible. This hat is for beauty. I want people to see it, and know that I have a beautiful new hat. I am always pleased when a friend tells me it is so beautiful that she would like to have one just like it.

There is a verse in the Book of Psalms which tells us that we should let the beauty of our Lord be seen in us. (Read Ps. 90:17.) Just as soon as you have asked the Lord Jesus to come into your heart to save you, you have become a Christian. Christ is in your heart and God the Father and the Holy Spirit are all in your heart and life to stay forever. With all the members of the Godhead living in us, our lives should be different from others who do not believe in Christ. Every place we go, every word we say, and everything we do should be different now that God is living in us.

We should let the beauty and loveliness of God shine out through us. Our smiles should be sweeter, our faces should show real joy, and the way we treat other people with kindness and thoughtfulness should let them know that we have Christ in our hearts. They should be able to see our cheerfulness even when we are sick or things go wrong. If we are mean and thoughtless, if we complain and criticize, or are selfish and dishonest, people will never know about our wonderful Saviour. Many **people** never go to church and few of them ever **read** the Bible. Watching what Christians **do and** say is the only way they can get an idea **of what** Christ is like.

Have your friends and schoolmates seen **the** beauty of God in you? Has your life been **so** sweet and different that they want to **have** Christ as their Saviour too? There is no joy like having someone say that he wants to **take** Christ as his Saviour because he has seen **what** a difference Christ has made in your life. **Just** think about it and ask God to help you show **His** beauty through you, so that you can win **others** to Christ.

FILLING OF THE HOLY SPIRIT

PREPARATION: Take a pair of white gloves and a Bible. Fill the fingers of the right glove over half full of soiled cotton.

PRESENTATION

I have a pair of white gloves with me this morning. I want them to remind us of some Christians I know. Suppose I tell that glove to pick up the Bible. Can it do it? It doesn't have any strength of itself to do anything.

We have already learned that when we ask the Lord Jesus Christ to save us, He comes into our hearts to live. The Holy Spirit comes into our hearts too, to help us live the kind of life that God requires of us. We are going to let my hand represent the Holy Spirit. (Use left-hand glove first.) The person this glove stands for has just taken Christ as his Saviour, and I am going to slip my hand into it to remind us that the Holy Spirit is now living in this Christian's heart. This glove doesn't have any more power to do what I tell it to than it did before I put my hand in it, does it? I am going to tell it to pick up the Bible. See, it does just what I have told it to do. What makes the difference? Of course, my hand is what is really picking up the Bible, but my hand is using the glove. We can't do anything more for the Lord now that we are Christians than we did before we were saved. God knew that, and that is why He sent the Holy Spirit to live in our hearts to do the work through us, just as my hand is working through the glove (Gal. 5:22, 23).

Now, I want to show you how the Holy Spirit works in the heart of this other Christian. (Put your right hand in the glove that has the cotton in the fingers.) I can't get my hand very far in the glove. When I tell this glove to pick up the Bible, it can't do it. There is something in the fingers of the glove that keeps me from getting my hand in it and picking up the Bible. Let's see what it is. It is just dirty cotton, but that makes us think of sin in our hearts. When we sin and don't confess it right away, it keeps

the Holy Spirit from having all of our hearts
and keeps Him from filling us. When we sin,
we grieve the Holy Spirit (Eph. 4:30). He has
to spend His time telling us that there is sin in
our hearts until we confess it. He can't fill us
and work through us until we confess that sin
(I John 1:9).

We will pretend that this person the glove
represents has listened to the Holy Spirit and
is telling God what he has done wrong. God
has forgiven him and washed away those sins.
We will remove the cotton now and see what
happens to this person. Now my hand will slip
all the way into the glove and I will try to get
it to pick up the Bible. It works just fine now,
because my hand has completely filled the glove
and my hand can pick up the Bible through the
glove. The only way we can be pleasing to God
is to keep sin out of our hearts. We must confess every sin the minute we realize we have
sinned. Then the Holy Spirit can have His way
in our lives and work through us to do God's
will.

LYING LABELS

PREPARATION: Buy a can of vegetables and a can of fruit the same size. Carefully take the label off one can and glue it over the label on the other can. Also take a can opener, a glass jar, and a tray. Only the can with the false label is used for the lesson.

PRESENTATION

This is a can that I bought at a grocery store. The label says it is a can of pears. Our government requires each company to put a label on all cans so we will know exactly what is in the can when we buy it.

We are told in the Bible that each Christian wears a label. There should be ways of knowing who is a Christian and who isn't by the way people live, shouldn't there? (Matt. 7:20.) Usually we ask them and they will say they have Jesus Christ in their hearts. Most Christians go to Sunday school and church too. They usually like to be with other people who are Christians. Can you think of some other ways we have of knowing a Christian? Yes, a Christian reads the Bible and prays.

Now, this can says that it is a can of pears. Let's open it now to see. (Open can and pour contents in glass jar so all can see a vegetable instead of pears. Work over a tray in case something should spill.) You are all surprised to see the corn, aren't you? We trust the labels on the cans we buy. Wouldn't your mother be surprised and provoked if something like this happened to her when she was getting dinner ready? This label is lying. Perhaps you children have guessed by now that I changed the label on the can. It was marked right when I got it at the store.

Boys and girls, there are many people who say that they are Christians when they really aren't. They are lying too. They may even go to Sunday school and church and read the Bible and pray. It is even possible for them to think they are Christians and be fooled. Satan likes to fool people into thinking that if they are trying to be good they are Christians. It doesn't matter what we say, or what we think, or even what we do, we aren't Christians unless we have asked the Lord Jesus Christ to come into our hearts to save us.

(Read I Sam. 16:7.) This verse tells us that man looks at the way people look on the outside and the way they act, but God can see right down into our hearts and He knows if we have taken the Lord Jesus Christ as our Saviour or not. You look very nice to me all dressed up, but I can't tell from looking at the outward appearance what is in your heart. Only you and God really know if you are a Christian. Is Christ there? If He isn't, please bow your head right now and ask Him to save you. He wants everyone to be saved (II Peter 3:9). He is happy when anyone will ask Him to come into his heart. All you have to do is ask, and He will do the rest for you. When Christ comes into your heart, He saves you and lives forever within your heart.

GOD'S CARE

PREPARATION: Secure an artificial bird, or picture; a wild flower; and a hair pulled from your head during the object lesson.

PRESENTATION

When the Lord Jesus Christ was here on the earth, He used three very unimportant and inexpensive objects to teach us about His care for us. I have brought these same objects with me this morning.

In many verses in the Bible, we are told not to worry. Everyone we know worries most of the time. Many people, even Christians, worry some of the time, but just because everyone worries that doesn't make it right or give us any excuse for worrying. God knew that this would be a very serious temptation to all of us, because He made so many wonderful promises in His Word to assure us that there is no reason for us to worry about anything.

(Show the bird or picture.) Christ said that when we look at the birds in the air who don't work or store up food, we should remember that God even takes care of them (Matt. 6:26). He said that five sparrows are sold for only one penny but not one of them is forgotten of God, and God knows when one falls to the ground (Luke 12:6). Have you ever tried to count all the birds you see? God cares for each one of them, and we are so much more important to God we can be sure that He will take care of us too.

(Pull a hair from your head.) Here is one little hair I just pulled from my head. God says that He cares so much for us that He even knows the number of hairs we have on our heads (Luke 12:7). If God cares enough to count the hairs on our heads, we can be sure He will meet our every need.

(Show a wild flower.) Christ told us to consider the lilies of the field. Lilies were a wild flower in Palestine, and there were fields of them that never had any care or special attention (Matt. 6:28-30). Then He said, if God takes care of the wild flowers and gives them such pretty colors even though they quickly die, can't you believe that He will take care of you? It is lack of faith to worry about anything in our lives. Christ says that when we worry we are acting like the unbelievers. God knows what we need even before we ask Him for things.

God has a plan for our lives. (Read Matt. 6:33.) He says that we should seek God and the things that concern Him first, and then He will take care of every need that we have. Isn't that wonderful? That is God's promise.

Christ used three things to teach us not to worry and to show us why there is no need to be concerned about the things we need. We are always in God's care, and He tells us to put all our care on Him because He loves us so much that He will take care of everything that concerns us (I Peter 5:7).

REFLECTORS

PREPARATION: Make a cardboard road sign with a beaded glass effect.

PRESENTATION

All of you have seen a road sign that looks something like this stop sign. The people who make these signs for the highway department put little beads of glass around the edge so the sign will show up well at night. In the daytime it is easy to see these signs, but at night it is much harder. These little glass beads don't have any light in themselves, but when a car light shines on them, it makes them look like they are lights. We call these reflectors. They reflect the light from an oncoming car, and shine the light back to the person who is driving. This way people can quickly see the sign and easily read what it says. If no car is coming with lights on, the glass beads are dark.

God's Word refers to us Christians as reflectors of God's love. (Read I John 2:15.) "If any man love the world, the love of the Father is not [reflected] in him." God says that we must not love the world. He does not mean the beautiful things He has made for us to enjoy, like the flowers and trees, the birds and squirrels, or the mountains and oceans. He wants us to enjoy the beautiful things that He has created. God doesn't want us to love the things that are evil and wrong and lead people into sin. Satan rules over this world and he does all he can to make us love the things that God hates. He wants us to disobey God and do things that displease God.

Now in this verse, God says that if we love the worldly things that Satan rules, we can't be "reflectors" of His love. You remember, we said that the glass beads don't have any light in themselves. They can only reflect the light that shines on them. Just so, we cannot put God's love in us. It is only as we let God reflect His love through us that we can love others as He loves them. It is only this way that we can be a witness and testimony to others that Christ died for their sins and by taking Him as Saviour they can be saved.

Let us be sure right now that we don't love things that we know are wrong and sinful and displeasing to God. If we do, God's love can't shine through us. You can't win others to Christ that way. If you know there is something wrong in your heart, now is the best time to confess that sin and let Him forgive you. Then God's love will be reflected through you and God can use you according to His will.

FISHING LURE

PREPARATION: Take some kind of fishing equipment, and a fly for catching fish.

PRESENTATION

How many of you boys and girls like to go fishing? What kind of equipment do you use to catch fish? I have some of my husband's equipment with me this morning. I have a fly here that is used to attract fish. You have to fool a fish by making it think that you are giving it something to eat. You cover a hook with a worm, or use a fly like this one so the fish will grab at it and be caught before it realizes you are trying to catch it. There has to be some kind of bait to catch fish.

Did you know that Satan has some wonderful bait to catch us in sin? He started in the Garden of Eden when he tempted Adam and Eve to eat of the fruit that God had forbidden them

to eat (Gen. 3:1-6). Adam and Eve were caught
by this bait and disobeyed God. They had to be
put out of the wonderful garden home, and
could never talk face to face with God again.
They had sinned by listening to Satan instead
of God.

Satan tried to tempt the Lord Jesus Christ in
the same way (Matt. 4:3-11). Three times he
tried to make attractive offers to Him, but
Christ is the sinless Son of God and He couldn't
fall into sin.

There is a verse (I John 2:16) that tells us
three ways that Satan will use to fool us into
sinning. Let me read it. Listen carefully so
you will be prepared when Satan comes with
his temptations. First, he makes us want to
have our own way by satisfying all our selfish-
ness. Second, he lets us see the things around
us that the unsaved people want to have. Then
he suggests ways that we can get them too, but
they are always wrong. Third, he puts a sinful
pride in us because of the things we have. He
makes having nice clothes and money and a
good position, success and education more important to us than doing God's will. Sometimes

he puts pride in our hearts because we are Christians and makes us feel that we are so much better than other people. He makes us want others to think we are more spiritual and godly than we really are.

God's Word tells us that Jesus Christ was tempted in "all points" just as we are, so He can help us when we are tempted to sin (Heb. 4:15). He has promised to help each one of us when Satan tries to get us to do wrong. He understands just how attractive Satan makes sin look, and how easy it is for us to take his bait. You can't keep from sinning in your own strength, but you can let Christ do it for you. Whenever you are tempted to do something wrong, remember how you fool fish to catch them. Then don't let Satan trap you by giving you some attractive bait to lead you on. Ask Christ to give you the power to refuse to go Satan's way.

ALL THINGS WORK TOGETHER FOR GOOD

PREPARATION: Secure a child's puzzle. A wooden one is best. Have the puzzle in pieces when the lesson begins.

PRESENTATION

This puzzle will show how God wants to work in our lives. Here are all of the pieces, but this way it doesn't make much sense. You can't tell what the picture is, can you? I'll try to put it together now. (Deliberately put it together wrong.) I want this piece to go here, and this piece here, but they don't seem to fit that way. The person who made this puzzle had a plan to follow. All the pieces must be put together in just the right places to make a perfect picture come out of this.

We are told in God's Word that He has a perfect plan for our lives. (Rom. 12:2.) Listen while I read a verse. So many Christian boys and girls and grown-up people think they have to work out the things in their lives. So many of us want things our own way and we aren't satisfied unless they work out just the way we plan. When we try to plan our lives, we make a mess of them as I did when I first started putting this puzzle together.

Everything that happens is important in making us just what God wants us to be. We can't understand why God doesn't send all pleasant things into our lives. It is hard to take when He sends a serious sickness, or we lose a loved one, or we fail in our school work. But God knows just the right things to send to make us into the kind of Christian boys and girls that He wants us to be. Every disappointment, every trial, every happy thing that comes into our lives is sent there by God because He knows that we need these things. You and I may not be able to see how His plan is working out for us right now, but someday we will see that He worked out every circumstance of our lives according to His will to make us more like Christ.

Rain is often unpleasant, but rain is necessary so that food, grass, and trees will grow, and so we will have water in our houses. Just so trials and disappointments are necessary to work out God's plan in our lives.

(Read Rom. 8:28.) We have this wonderful promise that everything God sends is for our good. This promise is given to "those who love God." Have you ever wondered if you love God as much as you should? But it is also promised to "those who are called according to his purpose," and that includes all Christians. If you have taken the Lord Jesus Christ as your Saviour, you are given this promise for your own. When we get to Heaven, we will understand why God works differently in every Christian's life. It would be so hard to take if we didn't know that God has control of our lives.

I know what picture is on this puzzle, as I planned this before I came. Now, I'll put it together and let you see it too. You and I don't have to struggle to put the circumstances of our lives together. God has the plan and He wants to work that out through us. We bring joy and glory to God when we are walking in His will. It is important that we want to do God's will with all our hearts, and He will see that His will is best for us.

God's first plan for everyone is to take Christ as Saviour, if you haven't done that before. Then He wants us to trust Him to work out His plan and will for our lives, believing that He will do what is best to make us more like Christ (Ps. 37:23).

TREASURES IN HEAVEN

PREPARATION: Secure some broken toys. Make two paper hearts the same size. Glue pictures of toys, TV, money, etc., on one, and glue pictures of Heaven, Bible, child praying, Christ, etc., on the second heart.

PRESENTATION

Here are a lot of broken, useless toys that my daughter at one time thought would make her very happy. But see what has happened to them. They are broken and we are going to throw them out. Now she wants something else. Have you ever told your mother that if you could just get that one thing you wanted you'd be happy and satisfied? Then she bought it for you and soon you saw something else that you wanted. You were so sure that if you could just have a new bike or a gun you'd never ask for anything else. But somehow you never seem to be completely satisfied. You children aren't the only ones; the grown-up people are like that too. A woman thinks that if she can only have a new house she'll be happy, but soon she wants something else. A man thinks that if he can just have a new car he'd never want anything else, but soon he does.

God tells us in His Word why we aren't satisfied. (Read Jer. 17:9). Our hearts are deceitful. They try to fool us by making us think that if we can only have things we want, we will be completely happy and never want anything else. But things can never fully satisfy.

Here I have a heart that is full of things. See the toys, TV and money, etc. There isn't room left for God and for the things that please Him. This heart wants only things for itself. Its only concern is satisfying all its selfish desires. But it is never satisfied.

Here is another kind of heart. This is the kind of heart that God wants us to have, the satisfied heart. We are told to set our affections, or love, on things in Heaven (Col. 3:2, 3). Right on top of this heart, we have put a picture of Heaven to show that this heart is more concerned about heavenly things that God likes than pleasing itself with earthly things. Christ said that where our treasures are, there will our hearts be also (Matt. 6:21). We can't love God and the Word if our hearts love selfish things more. God wants us to set our love on things that He loves.

This heart loves prayer, Bible reading, Sunday school and church and telling others about the Lord Jesus Christ. Above all it loves the Lord with all its heart, soul and mind. This is the only way we can have a happy, satisfied heart. Christ is the only One who can give the joy and peace we need. No amount of things like clothes, toys, TV and money will ever keep us satisfied, even if we have all we want. Set your love on Christ and the things that please Him, and you will have a happy, satisfied heart.

SEALED BY THE SPIRIT

PREPARATION: Secure a rubber stamp and a piece of paper.

PRESENTATION

Let me stamp this rubber stamp on this paper to show you what it says. It has my name, address, and telephone number on it. Just above that it says, "This is the property of ————." I stamp this on papers that I have written, on books that belong to me, and on the envelopes for letters I have written. Now everyone who sees this will know that this thing belongs to me. No matter where a book may be, or where a letter is sent, it always belongs to me. I wrote it and I have put my seal on it to show ownership.

You remember, I am sure, some of the Old Testament stories we have had. We learned that the kings of Israel used a seal for all the letters and laws they wrote. Once a king had put his seal on something it couldn't be broken. When Daniel continued to pray to God, even though he knew that the king had made a law that one could not pray to anyone but himself for thirty days, he was put in the den of lions. Even though the king liked Daniel and did all he could to save him, he could do nothing about it because he had made the law and put his seal on it. After Daniel was lowered into the den and the stone put over it, the king's seal was put on it and not even the king could break that seal. We know that God took care of Daniel and the lions didn't hurt him at all.

Each one of us who is a Christian has a seal put on him. We can't see the seal but we know that it is there because God said so. (Read Eph. 4:30.) Just as soon as we take the Lord Jesus Christ as Saviour He comes into our hearts, but something else happens too. The Holy Spirit seals us as God's property. That means that we will always belong to God and we can never be lost. This seal means that we are kept by the power of God and that nothing can separate us from God (Rom. 8:38, 39). Because Christ died for us, we will always belong to Him. Satan can never have us again. We have God's promise that we are His own here on the earth and when we die we will go to live forever with Him. If you have never asked Christ to save you, you still belong to Satan and don't have God's seal on you. Won't you let Jesus Christ come into your heart now? Then the Holy Spirit will seal you as one who belongs to God forever.

These papers and letters belong to me because I wrote them and have put my seal on them. We belong to God because the Lord Jesus Christ died to save us, and now we are sealed by the Holy Spirit to be God's property throughout all eternity.

PRAYER SHELF

PREPARATION : Secure a wooden spice shelf with three containers in it. (They can be bought at the dime store.) Print PRAYER SHELF on paper and glue on the bottom. Put one of the following words on each of the containers: YES—NO—WAIT. If there is room, print SEASON EACH DAY WITH PRAYER on paper and glue across the top. Have containers out of sight when lesson begins.

PRESENTATION

When I was a little girl, my mother had a big basement where she kept canned foods on shelves. She put fruit, vegetables, jams and jellies in jars to keep until we needed them. I like to think that God has a shelf in Heaven where He keeps the prayers of the saints in His jar (Rev. 5:8). God calls all Christians saints, so this verse is talking about all who have taken the Lord Jesus Christ as their Saviour. Did you realize that our prayers are kept by God and that they are an incense, or perfume, that goes up before the throne of God? How careful that should make us when we pray to God! Just any prayer won't do.

We are told to "pray without ceasing," and to "pray about everything." It is God's will that our lives be full of prayer. I have put this little sentence on the top of my prayer shelf. See, it says, "SEASON EACH DAY WITH PRAYER." It is commanded by God that we pray everyday.

I have brought three containers to put on this shelf to show how God answers our prayers. We often think that unless He gives us what we ask for, He hasn't answered our prayers. But that is not true as God has different ways of answering our prayers.

(Put the first container on the shelf.) Sometimes God has to say "no" to our prayers. He knows what is best for us, and in His love and wisdom He will refuse to give us something that He knows will hurt us. I won't let my little girl have a candy bar just before dinner because I know that she won't eat the proper things for dinner, and the candy often upsets her stomach. So God has to keep us from the things that would not be good for us. He does it because He loves us. Paul was one of the greatest Christians who ever lived. He was sick and asked God to heal him, but God said "no" to him (II Cor. 12:7-10). Instead of healing him, God promised that He would give him the strength and courage to keep on with his work in spite of this sickness.

(Put the next container on the shelf.) Sometimes, God says "yes" to the things we ask for, and He gives them to us right away. King Hezekiah was told by God that he was going to die. He prayed that God would let him live, and God answered his prayer by telling him that he would live another fifteen years. Sometimes, God will not only give us what we ask for but will give us more than we had hoped or expected (Eph. 3:20). If possible, when my girls ask for things I give them even more because I love them. So does our heavenly Father.

(Put the third container on the shelf.) Sometimes, God answers our prayers by telling us that we must "wait" for a while. For some reason that only God knows, it is best for us to wait until some later time to get the things we have asked for (Luke 18:7). Maybe, God waits to be sure that we really want them enough to keep praying for them. When Christ was here on earth, He told two parable-stories to teach us that we must keep right on praying even if we don't get an answer (Luke 11:5-10; 18:1-8).

It is a good idea to study your Bible to find all the verses where God promises to answer prayer. Then be sure to meet the conditions He has given, and you will have your prayers answered.

LEAVEN

PREPARATION: Take a loaf of bread and, if possible, a lump of dough. This can be made of flour and water.

PRESENTATION

Our object is something that you see in your home most of the time. It is a loaf of bread. This bread was made in a bakery. Does your mother ever make bread at home? Very few women make their own bread any more because it takes much time and it is so convenient to buy. I can remember that my mother made all the bread and rolls that our family ate when I was a little girl. I often watched her. She put flour, milk, egg, salt and some other things in the dough. She had to use yeast to make the bread rise, so it would be light and fluffy. One day, she forgot to put the yeast in the dough and the bread didn't rise and we couldn't eat it.

People have been making bread for many thousands of years. They believed that the rising of the bread was magic in those days. Now we know that yeast makes the starch turn to sugar and the sugar becomes gas. As the gas expands, it pushes the dough higher and higher.

Back in Bible days the people couldn't go to the store and buy yeast to make their bread rise like we can. Each time they made bread, they saved some of the dough like this (show the dough) to mix in with the next batch of dough for bread, and so on. The Bible calls yeast leaven. It was always used as an object to teach us a lesson about sin, and the way even a little sin spreads through our lives. Each year the children of Israel celebrated the Feast of the Passover. At that time, God commanded them to throw away all the old leaven of dough that they usually saved. They were to eat unleavened bread for a week. He was teaching them that they must put away all sin from their lives.

When Christ was living on earth, He often referred to leaven and always as a picture of sin. He told a parable-story of how a woman hid a little leaven, or yeast, in some dough, and before long it began to rise and expand until it had gone through all the dough (Matt. 13:33). Then He warned us that this was a picture of what would happen if we let any sin stay in our hearts. He warned us of leaven, to be careful not to let sin of any kind come into our lives (Matt. 16:6-12).

The action of the leaven in the bread dough shows us what will happen when we let any sin stay in our hearts. It will grow and expand and lead us into other sins. Just as the leaven gradually worked its way through the dough, sin will gradually affect our whole lives. It breaks our fellowship with God, it keeps us from having our prayers answered, it hurts God, and it makes it harder to have victory over other sins.

God's Word tells us what to do when we sin as Christians. (Read I John 1:9.) The minute we sin, we must tell God what we have done and He has promised to forgive us because Christ died for that sin. Don't wait until night, because you might forget what you did, and you will waste a day that you could have been in fellowship with the Lord.

GIVING

PREPARATION: Take a calendar, some dollar bills, and a lot of change.

PRESENTATION

This calendar will remind us of something that the Lord has asked every Christian to do at least once a week. I doubt if any of you can guess what I have in mind. Now, listen to a verse in God's Word. (Read I Cor. 16:2.) When is the first day of the week? (Refer to calendar.) It is Sunday; that is right. Then every Sunday, God says that we are to set aside some money for His work. If we don't do it every week, we might forget how much we should have given, or we might get so far behind that we don't have the money to catch up.

When you get ready to leave for Sunday school and church, do you get some of your own money to take, or does your father give you some money out of his pocket? Do you think it is God's will to give your daddy's money and save all of yours for yourself? What does the verse say? It says "every one of you," and Paul is speaking to Christians. So that means every one who belongs to the Lord Jesus Christ. Does that mean you? Yes.

Now, I would like to have a boy and a girl who get an allowance each week and, if possible, who have some way of earning money each week, to help me. Will you stand on each side of the table, please? We are going to use you two as an illustration of how we are to give to the Lord's work. Will you, Mary, tell me how much allowance you get each week? You get 25 cents. Do you have any way of earning money each week? You get 25 cents for washing the kitchen floor. All right, we will put two quarters here on the table beside you. Is that all the money you ever get? Sometimes you get some money for helping with the baby but not often. Now, Jim, how much allowance do you get? You get $1.00 a week. My, that is a big allowance! Do you have all of that for yourself, or do you have to buy something with that money? You have to buy your paper and pencils for school. Do you know how much that costs you? So, you spend about 25 cents a week for school supplies. Here is a $1.00 to put on the table beside you, but we had better take the 25 cents out of it, because that really doesn't belong to you, does it? The only honest thing to do is to use that money for your school supplies as your parents have told you to do. Do you have any way of earning money? You help deliver papers and get $2.00 for that. Let's add that $2.00 to your money.

Now, let's look at the two piles of money. Mary gets 50 cents each week and it can all be used for herself. Jim gets $2.75 a week all his own. How should each of them decide what they should give for the Lord's work? First, our verse says that we should give according to how much we have. That means that Jim should give more than Mary, doesn't it? We give in proportion to the amount of money that God has given us. Now, I want to read II Corinthians 9:7. This verse says that we are to decide in our own hearts what the Lord wants us to give. God is the only One who has the right to tell us what to give.

The verse also says that we must give cheerfully. That means that whatever we give is given because we love the Lord and really are happy to give to Him. Many people give to the church because they feel that they have to, or because they have promised to give a certain amount, but they don't really want to give it. God doesn't want that kind of giving. Suppose you gave your daddy a lovely gift and told him that you felt you had to give him something. Suppose you really didn't want to spend the money, as you had planned to use it for a baseball, and you were just giving him the gift because he had done so much for you. Do you think that your daddy would want that gift? It wouldn't mean a thing to him. He would much rather have you buy the baseball.

Maybe some of you don't receive an allowance and don't have any way of earning money. Then the only thing you can do is to give the money that your parents give you for Sunday school and church. From time to time, you will be given gifts of money, and then be sure that you give a part of that to the Lord.

I wish all of you would go home this morning and add up the money that you are given and the money you earn, and then ask the Lord how much of that He wants you to give for His work. After all, it is the Lord who enables us to get any money. It all really and truly belongs to Him. Then give it to Him cheerfully because you love Him. (If you feel that it is wise, you might have the two children decide before the others how much they should give.)

DEED TO A HOUSE

PREPARATION : Take the deed to your own house, or borrow one.

PRESENTATION

Here is the deed to the house I am living in now. Do you know what a deed is? I'll open it up and let you look at it while I tell you just what it is. There are a lot of words in this but what it all means is simple. This says that we have bought and paid for a house from ——— and it gives a description of the kind and size of the house and the lawn, and the number of buildings on the property. Then it says when we can move into the house. This proves that the house at 7007 Lakewood is mine. If anyone says that this house is not mine, I can prove that it is by showing the deed signed by my husband and the woman from whom it was bought. He bought the house so she couldn't get it back and neither could anyone else.

My husband looked for this house and bought it before I came here to live. I was so far away that I couldn't make the trip to see the house before the deed was signed. My husband wrote me letters describing what the house was like. He knows me so well that he knew just the kind of house I would like and which would meet the needs of our family. He described what the neighborhood was like, and what a nice school was nearby for our children. He thought this was the nicest house we could ever have. I read the letters over and over and dreamed about my new house in Dallas. I was anxious to come to Dallas to live in the house.

Before the Lord Jesus Christ went back to Heaven, He told His disciples that He was going to prepare homes for everyone who belonged to Him. Jesus Christ is preparing these homes for us Himself. These are wonderful new homes. Jesus Christ knows just the kind of heavenly home we will like and need. We have the wonderful promise that He is getting these homes ready and one day will come Himself to take us to that home. We can't see the home now, but He has written some letters to tell us a little about this heavenly home. These descriptions are written in the Bible. Let us read John 14:2, 3, 6. This gives us Christ's promise that He will make a home for us. Then in verse 6, He says that the only way we can get a deed to this home is to take the Lord Jesus Christ as our Saviour. He is the only way for us to get to Heaven. All you have to do is ask the Lord Jesus Christ to come into your heart. When you do that, Christ has promised you a home in Heaven with Him. He paid the price for your home in Heaven by dying on the cross for you, and now this home is given to you free. You don't need a deed like this one, because you have Christ's word that if you belong to Him, He will prepare a home for you, and He cannot lie! All the deed you need to a heavenly home is to have the Lord Jesus Christ in your heart. Christ's word is better than any deed you can get down here on earth.

THE BIBLE

PREPARATION: Secure a sponge and a pan of water. If possible, cut the sponge in a heart shape.

PRESENTATION

I have a sponge and a pan of water with me this morning. Do you know what a sponge is? It comes from a little animal that lives in the water. It is made of light, porous material which absorbs liquid. Will one of you come up here and put the sponge in the water? What happened? It is full of water, isn't it? If we had put the sponge in orange juice, it would be full of orange juice, and if we had put it in vinegar it would be full of vinegar. Whatever the sponge is put in, the sponge absorbs.

We are going to let the sponge represent the hearts of Christian boys and girls. That is why it is in the shape of a heart. Our hearts are something like the sponge because our hearts absorb whatever we put in them. There has to be something in our hearts; they don't just stay empty. If we put sin and selfish things in them, that is what will be there. If we fill them with the Word of God and love for the Lord, that is what will manifest itself to others. Other people know what we have in our hearts by the way we act.

We are going to let the water represent the Word of God. The Bible says that it acts like water in cleansing our hearts as we read and study it. Let me read you a verse (Eph. 5:26). Jesus Christ referred to the Word as water, when He talked to Nicodemus about how to be saved (John 3:5). In another verse, Jesus Christ said that we are made clean through the Word (John 15:3).

God gives us a very important reason for having our hearts full of His Word. (Ps. 119:11.) By reading and memorizing the Scriptures we can keep sin out of our hearts. There has to be something in our hearts, and unless we keep them full of the Bible they will be full of sin. When our hearts are full of the Word (water) there is no room for anything (sin) else. This sponge is so full of water that it can't absorb anything more. Even if you don't understand all that you read, or feel that you get a definite blessing from what you read, it is still very important to read the Bible because it has cleansing power in your life. The more we read the Bible and hear it taught, the easier it will be to keep from falling into sin and we will have less desire to sin.

Will one of you see what happens when this sponge heart is pressed and squeezed? Water comes out, doesn't it? Water comes out because that is what we put in it. If our hearts are full of the Word, the Word will come out when we have been unfairly treated, or put under some kind of trial or pressure. If our hearts are full of self and sin, we will say mean things when we are pressed or have trouble with others. We will be resentful and unhappy when we go through trials.

The Bible should have first place in everyone's life daily. First, it makes us "wise unto salvation" (II Tim. 3:15). Then after we are Christians, it shows us the sin in our lives and how to confess it. It also teaches us about God, and helps us "grow in grace, and in the knowledge of our Lord and Saviour Jesus Christ" (II Peter 3:18).

CHRISTIAN LIGHTS

PREPARATION : Secure light bulbs, sizes 7½, 50, and 150 watts, and an extension cord. Connect cord to an electrical outlet.

PRESENTATION

Here are three light bulbs, and we are going to let them represent Christian boys and girls. As I put each of them on this extension cord they will shine, showing that they have the Light of the world, the Lord Jesus Christ, in their hearts as their Saviour. We are told as Christians that we are to shine for Christ that others may see our good works and glorify our Father who is in Heaven. This is the way we can be a testimony to others of what Christ can do for people when they let Him come into their hearts.

If you look closely at the top of these lights, you will see some numbers and words on them.

This one says 7½ watts; this one says 50 watts; and this one says 150 watts. That means that each of these lights gives out a different amount of light when it is connected to the electricity. The company that makes these lights stamps on top the amount of light they will give, so that when we buy them we will know how much light to expect.

God has given each one of us who are Christians different talents and abilities to work for Him, and He puts us in different places to serve Him. He doesn't expect children to do what a Sunday school teacher can do, or a young person to be a minister. He only wants each of us to do His will. He wants each of us to be faithful wherever He puts us to work.

Now let's turn on these lights. The 7½-watt bulb is giving out only a little light, but it is giving out all the light it can. It was made only to give out 7½ watts. I use this little bulb as a night light in the hall, so we can see to move around at night. I don't want any more light there or it would keep us awake at night. This is the only place where I can use this bulb, as it wouldn't give out enough light for reading or working.

Now let's put the 50-watt bulb in the socket and see how much light it gives. This one gives more light and it, too, gives out all that it can. I use this one in my clothes closet. My closet is very dark and I can't see anything in it unless this light burns. I don't use it often, and it is seldom seen by anyone else, but it is very necessary. Suppose this bulb says, If I can't shine all the time and be seen by others, I won't shine at all. I would have to grope around in the darkness if this bulb didn't burn. Wouldn't it be a shame if someone is walking in the darkness of sin, because you might have felt like this bulb and refused to shine so they would know about the Lord Jesus Christ?

Now let's see the 150-watt bulb. That gives out much more light. Wouldn't it be strange if this light refused to give out any more light than the 7½-watt bulb? I use this one in my living room where we need a lot of light to read and sew, talk and study. The other two bulbs wouldn't give out enough light for these things.

Each of these bulbs has a proper place to shine and a proper amount of light to give out.

God has a plan for each one of us, whether young or old. The only way He can use us is for us to do just what He wants us to do, in the way and place He wants us to do it. If God has made you like the 7½-watt bulb, you must shine just as brightly as you can. If you are a 50-watt bulb, or a 150-watt bulb, you must shine to full capacity as God planned. It isn't important how much light you can give. What is important is to give out the amount of light that God has given you. Your job is to shine for Him where He puts you to be a witness to others about the Lord Jesus Christ.

MEMBERS OF CHRIST'S BODY

PREPARATION: Take a hammer.

PRESENTATION

My husband is building a den on the side of our house, so the children will have a playroom and a place to watch television. This is the hammer he was using to drive the nails into the boards. Last week, he missed a nail and hit his thumb. It hurt terribly and swelled up almost twice its usual size. He didn't do it on purpose; it was an accident.

I am going to hold this hammer up now and put my other hand under it. If I tell you I am going to hit my thumb as hard as I can, will you believe me? You are right. Why don't you think I'll hit my thumb? Why, of course, it would hurt. My hand is connected to my arm, and my arm to my body, and even though it is

a very small part of my body, it will hurt. We
don't deliberately hurt ourselves, do we?

(I Cor. 12:12-31.) God's Word tells us that
as each of us takes the Lord Jesus Christ as
Saviour, He makes us members of Christ's
body. You are a part of Christ's body, and I
am a part of Christ's body, and all Christians
are a part of His body. (Read I Cor. 12:12,
13a, 27.) We don't know what part God has
made us, but the Bible tells us that we are all
equally important to Him. It says that when
one Christian suffers, we all suffer because we
are all in one Body (I Cor. 12:26).

When anyone of us does anything to hurt another Christian, we are really hurting Christ
and ourselves, just as the hammer would hurt
all of me even though I hit only my thumb. Perhaps you think that you have never done anything to hurt another Christian, because you
haven't hit him with your fist or a stone, or
tripped him. (Mention some things that you
have seen members of your group doing.)

There is one way that we have all hurt each
other, and that is by the use of our tongues.
The Book of James (ch. 3) tells us how much

trouble our tongues can make for other Christians. Have you ever lied about another Christian? Have you said mean, unkind things to another Christian that would make that one feel hurt? Have you lost your temper and told someone just what you thought of him? There are many more ways that you can cause Christians to suffer by the things you say that aren't true, or are unkind and shouldn't be said. God's Word says that tongues are like fire and are full of iniquity or sin (James 3:6). Only the Lord Jesus Christ can control our tongues and keep us from saying the wrong things. Remember, the next time you are tempted to say something false about a Christian that you are not only hurting him but you are hurting Christ and yourself, because we are all members of Christ's body.

BABY FOODS

PREPARATION: Take a nursing bottle with milk in it, a jar of strained baby food, and a colored picture of cooked meat and other tempting foods.

PRESENTATION

How many of you boys and girls have a baby at your house? I know that some of you do, or have seen someone taking care of a baby. I brought a bottle of milk and some baby food with me this morning. I wonder if any of you would like to have these foods for your dinner tonight? Don't worry, I know that you wouldn't. Once we begin to grow up, this kind of food is tasteless and uninteresting and none of us would like this warm, sweet milk that we would have to suck out of a nipple.

I have a picture of a wonderful meal. This

is what each of us would rather have for our dinner. Look at that meal and those tempting desserts! Once we get off baby foods and eat meals like this one, we know how good grown-up food is and we never want to go back to baby food again.

In some verses in the Bible, we are told that God's Word is something like the foods we eat. For the new Christians, we are told that the Bible is like milk (I Peter 2:2). There is so much in the Bible that even the youngest Christian can understand, because the Holy Spirit teaches us what is in the Word. Then the Bible tells us that it is like well-cooked meat to the Christian who has grown in the Lord (Heb. 5:13, 14; I Cor. 3:2). In another verse, we are told that the Bible is sweet like honey.

Have you ever wondered what would happen if a person had baby food and milk all his life? He wouldn't grow. He would be sick because he wouldn't eat enough food and finally would die of starvation.

If our bodies grew in proportion to the amount we read the Bible, I am afraid that most of us would still be just babies. Maybe our souls and spirits are dying of spiritual starvation. That is why we live such unhappy Christian lives, and have so little victory over sin. We always want three meals a day to keep our bodies satisfied, but most of us don't see the need of feeding our souls on the Word of God. Once we get a taste of the wonderful depths of God's Word and see how it makes us grow spiritually, I am sure we will never be satisfied to go back to a life of forgetting to read God's Word, any more than we would be willing to go several days at a time without eating any food.

Christ said: "Blessed are they which do hunger and thirst after righteousness: for they shall be filled" (Matt. 5:6). He means that if we really want to read the Word and pray everyday, we will be happy and satisfied. If you haven't been reading the Bible as you should, why don't you pray that God will make you just as anxious to read the Bible everyday as you are to eat your meals? God has made this promise, and if we keep our part He has promised to make us happy and full, and that we will "grow in grace, and in the knowledge of our Lord and Saviour Jesus Christ" (II Peter 3:18).